Teaching an
Algonkian
Language as a
Second Language

A Core Program
for Kindergarten

© Published under authority of the
Hon. J. Hugh Faulkner,
Minister of Indian and Northern Affairs,
Ottawa, 1978
QS-5096-000-EE-A1
Catalogue No. R42-1/ 2
ISBN 0-662-10175-8
Design Management: Eric Plummer
Production: J.-Y. Pigeon
Design: Eiko Emori

Contents

This course has been written and field-tested by members of the Native Language Project Teams, Ontario Region, Department of Indian and Northern Affairs, 1974—76. It is presented in the hope that, increasingly, children will learn to speak their native language with fluency and enjoyment.

Basic Method
(read carefully)

- Use *only* the native language in the classroom. English should be used only in extreme emergencies.
- Talk naturally, *as if* the children understood the native language, but by gestures, pictures, and all means possible, *show* them the meaning of what you are saying.
- Use much more language than what is written for each lesson. The special language in each lesson indicates what the child should actually learn that day, but you must say much more than this (casually) to build a language background for the children.
- Do not insist that the children *speak* the native language. Your goal is that they *understand* you and respond to what you are saying. They can show they understand by:
    Nodding or shaking their heads
    Doing what they are asked
    Answering in English
    Answering in the native language
- If the children *do* speak the native language, show how pleased you are. But accept any of the other ways that show they understand. They'll have plenty of opportunity to speak the native language in grade one and up.
- Keep your class interesting, lively, and a *happy* place to be. It is important to build in the children a good feeling about using the native language.

Suggestions for the Teacher*

Organization of the Course

1. Units

Read the *whole* unit over before starting to plan any of the lessons you will teach in the unit. Each unit is written around an *interest topic,* and has one or more *structural items* and a recommended *time period.*

The *interest topic* provides something to talk about, and to do things with. We can't "talk about talking"; we talk about real things. The more interested the children become in the topic, the less self-conscious they will be about the language they are learning. The less self-conscious they are, the more effectively they will learn the language. So develop your topic well enough to capture and hold each child's interest.

The mastery of *structural items,* as given in the *teaching points* at the beginning of each unit, should be your goal for each unit. Mastery of specific vocabulary is *not* a primary goal. At the conclusion of each unit, evaluate your teaching on the basis *not* of how many new words the children have recognized, but on the basis of how well they handle the *structures* you have been teaching.

Plan to stick to the *time period* as closely as possible. If you go one or two days over or under once in a while it is not too serious, *but* if you are continuously taking more or less time than is indicated, you may wish to take a serious look at your teaching methods and adjust them accordingly. Less than the recommended time will not give enough practice with any given structure. More than the suggested time will exhaust the children's interest in the topic, and lack of interest makes for bad language learning.

2. Sections

Within each unit are several sections, and each section is numbered. There are 78 sections in all in the kindergarten course. These sections are *not* intended to be lessons. They are *steps* to be followed in teaching the unit. Some steps are easy, and you may want to have two or even more sections in one lesson. Other steps are more involved, and it may take several lessons to cover them.

In planning a unit, decide what proportion of your time you want to spend on each section. Then, on the basis of total time allotted to the unit, write beside each section the amount of time you will spend on it.

Sections are numbered continuously through the whole year so that it will be easy to refer back to previous sections for review, and so on. It is suggested that you keep a page somewhere in your plan book on which you record each review of the sections. This page might be organized something like this:

Section 1	Section 2	Section 3	Section 4
P. Sept. 5	P. Sept. 6	P. Sept. 8	P. Sept. 10
R. Sept. 7	R. Sept. 12	R. Sept. 30	R. Sept. 12
R. Oct. 4	R.	R.	R.
R.	R.		
Section 11	Section 12	Section 13	
P. Sept. 15	P. Sept. 15	P. Sept. 17	
R.	R.		
R.			

In this sketch, "P" stands for the initial presentation, and "R" for review. By keeping a page such as this, you can see at a glance what sections need further review.

You will notice that a number of sections in each unit are devoted to two special kinds of review: integration and consolidation. Integration lessons seek to take material just learned and integrate (or join and apply) it with material previously learned. Consolidation lessons seek to take material just learned and use it in various ways to strengthen the children's ability to handle it.

---

*Note: For a list of terms used in this course, see the Glossary, page 58.

3. Lessons

It is up to the teacher to plan each lesson. It is strongly recommended that a daily record of lesson plans be kept.

Since choice of much of the vocabulary to be used is left to the teacher, it is also important to keep accurate records of the vocabulary that actually has been chosen. In selecting vocabulary, choose words that are:

Easy enough for your children to master
Interesting enough to make them *want* to learn
Useful enough for them to practise outside of class.

4. Adjusting the Course

This course is designed to be taught in 30 weeks. The average school year is about 38 weeks, but often the native language teacher loses time at the beginning and end of the school year, and at Christmas and spring breaks. Therefore, depending on *your* circumstances, the course may need to be shortened or lengthened a little.

In addition, no two classes are exactly alike. Some will learn quickly, and you may find the course is a little too easy for them. For other classes, the course may be a little too difficult, because of lack of language background, shyness, lack of opportunity to practise language outside of school, and so on.

For reasons of time or class ability, then, you may wish to adjust the course slightly. What are some ways this may be done?

● To lighten the course, reduce the amount of vocabulary taught. Do *not* omit structures. To enrich the course, add more items of vocabulary, without changing the structures. For example, in Unit 5, vocabulary could be adjusted thus:

Regular Unit
  mother
  father
  grandma
  grandpa
  older brother
  older sister
  younger sibling
Simplified Unit
  mother
  father
  younger sibling
Enriched Unit
  mother
  father
  grandma
  grandpa
  older brother
  older sister
  younger sibling
  father's sister
  mother's brother
  (cross) cousin

● To further lighten the course, omit the following sections: 11, 20, 28, 35, 46, 50, 70, 71.

● To further enrich the course, teach the *Language Enrichment* portions as extra sections. Teach little songs whose language structures and vocabulary complement the lessons, or put together dramas, using structures being learned.

Preparing to Teach This Course

1. Preparation of Language Materials

It is likely that a number of the English sentences given in this course will sound awkward or even ridiculous in your dialect. Be sure to let your good sense tell you how to adjust the language of the course so that what you teach sounds like normal everyday speech in your community. Some *Language Notes* are scattered throughout the course for your guidance, but where you run into a language problem and there's no note for it, be guided by your own feeling for the language. This course is intended as a guide, and to give suggestions; it is not a list of unchangeable rules to follow.

It would be most useful to go through the whole course by yourself or with another fluent speaker, marking necessary language changes, before beginning to teach.

2. Preparation of Teaching Materials

A list is given on page 56 of all materials you will need. Collect those things that you can obtain and put them in boxes labelled according to the unit in which you will use them.

● Pictures

There are pattern pictures given in this book for some of the picture cutouts you will need. All of these must be enlarged before you can use them. As a general rule, the larger you make them the more effective they will be as teaching tools.

To adapt: Make any changes you wish in the drawings. The nearer the pictures are to local familiar things the better. For instance, the buildings for Unit 6 could be adjusted to look like buildings in your community.

To enlarge: Trace the picture onto an overhead acetate sheet. Project the acetate onto the wall with the overhead projector. Move the projector toward or away from the wall until the picture is the size you need. Then put your paper on the wall and trace the picture.

To finish: Use heavy cardboard whenever possible. A good method is to make your picture on Bristol board and then glue this with rubber cement to heavy-duty corrugated cardboard. Use felt pens to colour your pictures. Colouring should be bold and bright. Some teachers like to spray their finished work with urethane to give it a hard, wipe-proof finish. (*Warning:* if you plan to spray with urethane, use *water soluble* felt pens; urethane dissolves waterproof inks.) Wherever possible, cut out the shapes of the pictures. For the pictures in Unit 9, dotted lines suggest cutting lines so figures will stand and balance well.

● Talking Books

These are important to your teaching. See pages 36 to 49, for pictures and tape scripts. To make talking books, enlarge and colour each picture as indicated above, one picture to one sheet of light-coloured Bristol board. Attach all Bristol board pages together in order by using plastic rings at the left side of each big page to form a book. Next, record the dialogue for each book. Make sure it is clear and natural sounding — not too fast and not too slow. Use various voices to give a conversational effect when this is indicated. Record a little signal (a fork hitting a water glass is good) to show when it's time to turn the page. If possible, use cassette tapes so the children can use them themselves later on.

It is also recommended that in addition to the big classroom talking book, small individual talking books be made. These can be used at activity centres with a listening station or sent home with the children *after* they have learned the language in the book. To make small books, enlarge each picture to an 8½ x 11 inch size, run off a number of copies, and staple pages together or punch and place in binders.

3. Preparation of Support Materials — Songs

Short, simple songs are a great help to the language teacher. Try to remember, collect, or compose songs to be included in your course. The best songs are the ones that repeat the vocabulary and structures you are teaching and do not bring in too much *new* language. For instance, for Unit 1, a song like the following would be excellent:

Hello, hello
Hello girls
Hello boys
Hello, hello, hello.

Or, for Unit 10:

The bears went for a walk
The bears went for a walk
Little girl came in
The bears went for a walk.

If you do think of useful songs, it might be helpful to record them on tape with someone talented on the guitar or piano. The tapes would then always be available to reinforce your language teaching.

4. Preparation of Community Materials

Although this step is not essential, it is recommended as an excellent way to enlist and hold community support for your program. Prepare a brief outline, to be sent home to the parents at the end of each unit, with a list of the sentences and vocabulary that the children have been learning in that unit. These summaries can help you in several ways, such as:

● Preventing parents who don't know the language from feeling left out

● Showing parents who do know the language how they can best help their child at home (without expecting too much or too little from him)

● Demonstrating to everyone that your course is important, and showing them just how seriously you are working at it.

Keep a copy of this summary in your plan book. You'll find it helpful to look back on.

Note: It might also be useful to notify parents ahead of time about the safety warnings on medicines (Unit 9) and matches (Unit 11).

Outline of the Kindergarten Course

Unit 1 (two weeks)
Getting to Know You
- Common classroom expressions
- Children's names

Unit 2 (two weeks)
Let's Eat Together
- TA and TI imperatives
- Common foods

Unit 3 (two weeks)
Where Things Are
- Locatives
- Household furniture

Unit 4 (three weeks)
Our Pet
- 3rd person independent — AI verbs
- Negative and yes/no question forms
- Forest animals' names

Unit 5 (four weeks)
My Family
- 1st, 2nd, 3rd person possessives (kinship)

Unit 6 (three weeks)
My Community
- 1st, 2nd, 3rd person possessives
(regular animate and inanimate nouns)
- Common places (buildings and geographical terms)
- Weather terms

Unit 7 (two weeks)
The Clothes I Wear
- TA and TI verbs and/or noun incorporation
- Clothing

Unit 8 (three weeks)
Good Morning!
- 1st and 2nd person independent verbs
- Body parts (possessive forms)

Unit 9 (three weeks)
Community Helpers
- TA verb forms (3 on 4)
- Negative forms — imperative and
independent

Unit 10 (four weeks)
Let's Put On a Play
- Voluntives, diminutives, past tense

Unit 11 (two weeks)
What Do Things Do?
- AI, II, TA and TI verb forms

Unit 1
Getting to Know You

Time
Two weeks

Teaching point
Common classroom expressions

Purpose
- To give the teacher and pupils opportunity to know each other.
- To learn the "ground rules" for language time.
- To establish a warm, happy climate where language learning can be fun.

Material needed
- One hand puppet (preferably a "Native" puppet).

Language

1. **Hello**
   My name is_____.
   What's your name?
   What's his name?
   His name is_____.
2. **Yes, no**

3. **Me, you, him**

4. Singular and plural imperative forms for:
   stand, sit, turn around, jump, come
5. **Here, there**

6. **Boy, girl,**
   boys, girls

Suggested Activities

1. Teacher can tell his or her own name to class and use hand puppet to introduce other responses. Give the puppet a name also. The classroom teacher might assist you ahead of time by pinning children's names on their clothing.
2. (a) Continue to use hand puppet. Play a game similar to "Button, button, who's got the button", using a penny. Ask puppet: Does Tom have the penny? No. Does Jane have the penny? Yes, etc.
   (b) Is your name Bob? No.
   Is his name Andy? Yes, etc.
3. (a) Continue to play the penny game. Ask: Who has the penny? Answer: You, me or him.
   (b) Ask: Who is Jane? Answer: You or me.
   (c) Ask: Do you (do I, does he) have it? Answer: Yes, etc.
4. Have class obey instructions both as a group and individually. It will be fun for them if the puppet gives the instructions from time to time.
5. Let one child hide.
   (a) Ask puppet first, then children: Where is John? Answer either: Here or there.
   (b) Ask: Is John here? Yes or no. Is John there? Yes or no.
   Note: Take care that "here" is used only for things close to the speaker, and "there" only for things at some distance from the speaker.
6. Puppet may tell the teacher about all the children in the class, for example: Sally is a girl; Bob is a boy, etc.

(a) Repeat activity 4, with boys: stand; girls:
turn around, etc.
(b) Ask puppet: Is Jane a boy? etc.

Language Note for Section 6: There will likely
be several different ways to say this in your
language. Choose one way to begin with, and stick
to it until the children are completely familiar
with it. Then gradually introduce the other ways,
one at a time, as you feel ready to do so. Remember,
the children don't have to ask the question: they
need only *understand* it, and answer Yes or No.

Unit 2
Let's Eat Together

Time
Two weeks

Animate and inanimate nouns in TA and TI
imperatives

● Paper plates and cups, plastic knives,
forks, spoons.
● Play food *or* pictures of food cut from magazines
and pasted onto the paper plates.
 In selecting the foods to teach, limit yourself
to only the number you think your class can
reasonably handle, choose foods that they
actually eat from day to day in their own homes,
and try to select about half animate items and
half inanimate ones.
 A table and a small cupboard would also
be useful.

7. **Bring the** *(animate food)*

8. **Bring the** *(inanimate food)*

9. **Bring the** *(mix animate
 and inanimate foods)*

10. Integration

11. **Bring the knife, fork, spoon,
 cup, plate**

12. **Put it here.
 Put it there.
 Put the_____on the table.
 Put away the_____.
 Thank you**

7. Have the children bring you, on plates, the various
 objects you ask for.

8. Put away all animate foods for the first
 presentation of inanimate ones.

9. Class may sit in a circle and pretend to be having
 a feast, passing food to each other on request.

10. Who has the meat? Jane, you, me, etc.
 Is this bread? Yes, no.
 Where is the potato? Here, there.

11. If each child has a set of paper and plastic
 tableware, he can hold up each item, as you name it,
 for vocabulary drill. Be sure, however, to end
 with the full sentence, "Bring the_____", acted out.

12. The children can dramatize a whole meal, setting
 the table ("Come to the table"), passing things and
 pretending to eat, tidying up afterward.

For quick-learning classes, some of these phrases
could also be added.

Bring the soap.	Put flowers in the cup.
Bring a towel.	Put food on the plate.
Eat the (food).	Put water in the cup.
Drink water.	Put soap in the water.
Bring flowers.	Fetch the_____.

Unit 3
Where Things Are

Time

Two weeks

Teaching point

Locatives

Materials needed

● Talking book: Where's Kitty? (See page 36).

● Toy box (a cardboard carton will do — so much the better if it's attractively decorated) with about six toys in it. In selecting the toys, try to choose about half animate and half inanimate ones, and be sure they are the same kinds of toys the children play with at home. Also ensure that both boys and girls will find something of interest in the box. One toy should be a large rubber ball.

Language	**Suggested Activities**
13. Talking book	13. (a) Show talking book: Where's Kitty? Go through the book two or three times. The children may enjoy making a choral response "No" with the tape, as they become familiar with it. (b) If possible, act out the story in the classroom, using a toy cat, toy stove, etc.
14. Game: hide the toy	14. Have one child cover his eyes while the class hides one of the toys (name it) from the box. (a) Teacher asks child who is "it" a variety of questions: Is the ball on the chair? Is it behind the cupboard? etc. Teacher indicates place meant while asking each question. "It" replies yes or no. (b) When class becomes proficient at this, play the game in the same way but *without* indicating the places, as named. **Note:** It might be helpful, the first time the game is played, to have puppet be "it".
15. Integration	15. (a) Include here and there in previous activities: for example, here, on the table; there, near the door, etc. (b) Action chains (intransitive): for example, stand up, go to the window, turn around, come here, sit down, etc. (c) Who is *behind the door?*, etc. You, me, him, Johnny. (d) Action chains (transitive): bring the *bread*, *ball*, etc. Put it on the table. Put away the *dishes*, etc.

16.   Game: to whom?

16.   (a) Children sit on floor in large circle. Teacher asks: Who wants the ball? When a child says "me", teacher rolls the ball to him and asks again: Who wants the ball? When another child says "me", teacher tells the first child: Roll the ball to *Tommy*. Game proceeds in this way.

(b) Game can be varied by using other toys from the box. Teacher can say: Give the doll to Janie, etc.

Language Note for Section 16: If there is no single verb meaning roll in your language, use any suitable verb, for example, send, or push.

Unit 4
Our Pet

Time

Three weeks

Teaching points

3rd person independent (AI) verbs

Negative forms and yes/no question forms

Names of forest animals

Materials needed

● A small pet in a cage (mouse, hamster, gerbil, rabbit or similar) and pet's needs.

● Talking book: Forest Animals (See page 39).

Language	Suggested Activities
17. **The mouse is sleeping,** etc. (at least four other verbs describing what animal habitually does).	17. Introduce pet to the class and let them observe it. Watch the mouse, and say aloud what it is doing, using verbs: eat, sleep, scratch, run, drink, etc. Repeat each verb as often as opportunity arises until children are familiar with these words.
18. **Is the mouse sleeping?** etc.	18. Ask questions using the verbs taught, and have children reply yes or no.
19. **Yes, he's sleeping.** **No, he's not sleeping.**	19. Continue as in Section 18, but repeat the child's reply using language indicated.
20. **Yes, the mouse is sleeping.** **No, the mouse is not sleeping.**	20. Continue as in Section 19, but include the noun.
21. Integration	21. Bring water for the mouse (or food, etc.). Where is the mouse? Is the mouse a girl? A boy? What's the mouse's name? Who will clean the cage? You, me, him, John. Put the cage on the floor. Put away the food.
22. Integration	22. (a) Do not bring pet to class. Use the verbs the children have learned by letting individuals act them out. From these, develop sentences such as: Timmy is sleeping. Is Janie eating? No, Dianne isn't running. (b) It should be an easy step from Section 22 (a) to develop the imperative forms of these verbs: sleep! eat!, etc.
23. Plural forms	23. Show talking book: Forest Animals. Go through the book a number of times until children are familiar with the plural forms.
24. **The boys are sleeping,** etc. **The girls are sleeping,** etc. Negatives Interrogatives (yes/no)	24. (a) Proceed with similar method to Section 22 (a), but use groups of students (for example, girls and boys) to develop plural forms. b) As in Section 22 (b), develop plural imperative forms.

Language Note for Section 21: There are various possible ways to say "his cage". One simple one might be "his home".

Language Note for Section 22 (a): It may be natural to you, as a native speaker, to want to use the form here meaning "pretending to sleep" rather than "sleeping". To make it simpler for the children, however, it would be better to stick to the simple form "sleeping" for now.

Language Enrichment

For quick-learning classes, some of these phrases could also be added:
Be careful!
Be gentle!
Don't scare him!
Don't be noisy!
His tail is long.
He's soft.
He's pretty.

Unit 5
My Family

Time
Four weeks

Teaching points

1st, 2nd, 3rd person possessives (kinship)

Materials needed

- Large sheets of newsprint and tempera paint
- Family photographs
- Peep show box
- Dress-up clothes

Notes on Materials: If possible, ask the classroom teacher to help you prepare materials for this unit. Each child in the class should paint, on *large* newsprint sheets, a picture of himself and his family. Since the art of children of kindergarten age is not always easy to interpret, it would be helpful to have each member of the family labelled at the time the child paints the picture.

In addition to their doing these paintings, each child should be encouraged to bring in family photographs. This project might start at least a week ahead of the date you intend to use the photos, which could be pinned on the classroom bulletin board as they come in. Each child's name should be printed next to the photos he has brought.

A peep show can be made from a shoebox. Cut a large hole in the lid, and cover with white tissue paper to let the light through. Cut an eyehole at one end. At the other end, cut a slot so that various picture cards can be dropped in. Leave the lid loose so that objects can be easily added and removed.

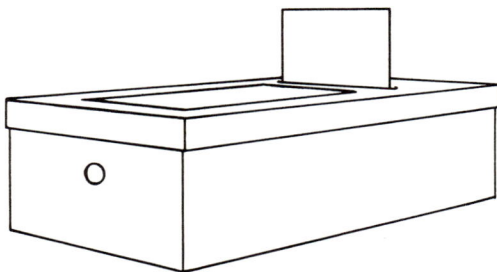

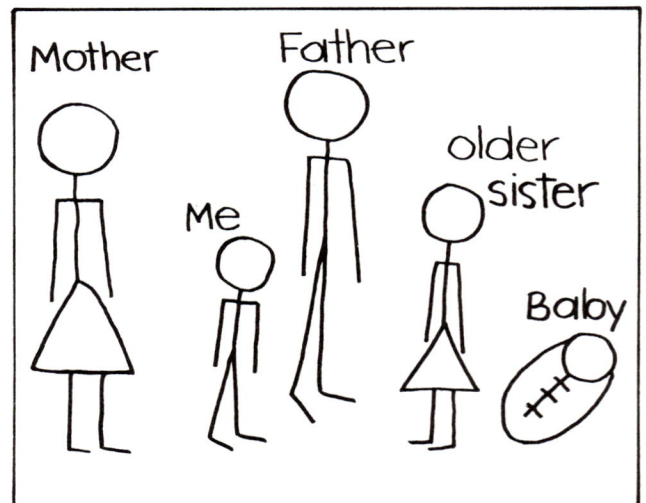

Language	**Suggested Activities**
25. 1st, 2nd, 3rd person possessive forms of **mother, father**	25. (a) Puppet looks at the children's paintings. Starting with "his mother", puppet points to various paintings, and says: Here is Tommy's mother; here is Jane's mother, etc. (b) Puppet then "paints" a picture, and says: Here is my mother. Teacher (to puppet): Is this your mother? Puppet: Yes, this is my mother. Teacher (to class): This is (*puppet's name*)'s mother. (c) Proceed in the same way with the term "father".
26. Integration	26. (a) Pointing to a picture (on painting or photograph), teacher asks: Whose mother is this? Mine, his, etc. (b) Where is Tommy's father? Here, there. (c) What's your mother's name? (This may prove impossible: it depends on local custom how well parents' names will be known to the children.)
27. 1st, 2nd, 3rd person possessive forms of **grandmother, grandfather**	27. Proceed in the same way as for Sections 25 and 26.
28. New verb vocabulary (stress AI verbs)	28. Working from family photographs, comment on activities you see. For instance: My father is getting in (to a vehicle). Your grandma is reading, etc.
29. 1st, 2nd, 3rd person possessive forms of **older sister, older brother, younger sibling**	29. Proceed in the same way as for Sections 25 and 26. **Note:** Section 26 (c) should work well here. The children will all like to tell you the names of their siblings. It will be important, at this point, to *ensure* they understand these terms. You may do so by writing (previously, with the classroom teacher) the names and relative ages of the siblings on the children's artwork. Avoid later confusion by preventing any errors *now*. In each case, teach 1st and 2nd person possessive forms before teaching 3rd person possessive forms.
30. Integration	30. Using the kinship terms, and verbs from Unit 4 and from Section 28 of this unit, practise as many combinations as possible. Include interrogative and negative forms.
31. 1st and 2nd person on 3rd person animate (See *Glossary:* Subject-Object Combinations)	31. Use the children's own photographs in the peep show box. (a) Ask: Do you see John? Yes, no. (b) Ask: Whom do you see? John. (c) Ask: Do you see Tommy's mother? Yes, no. **Note:** Remember that the puppet can "look" too, and will be a good model for the children to follow.

32. 1st and 2nd person on 3rd person inanimate

32. Select a number of inanimate objects previously learned (for instance, from toy box in Unit 3), and play the peep show game with them, asking: What do you see?

Note: To keep the whole class interested while one person looks into the box, teacher should show the whole class (except the one who will look) what is being put in. This will increase interest, and also ensure best exposure to the language being used.

33. 1st and 2nd person on 3rd person (animate and inanimate)

33. Mix animate and inanimate objects in the peep box.

Language Note for Section 31 (c): Since this sentence uses an obviative form for mother, it may be a little confusing to the children. If you feel they will have trouble with it at this point, leave it out now and come back to it later in the year.

Language Enrichment
For quick-learning classes:
I accompany (him).
I make (it, him). (Use plasticene and let children make objects already learned.)
I like the taste of (it, him).
I eat (it, him).
I drop (it, him).
These verbs may be practised with the appropriate animate and inanimate nouns previously learned.

Unit 6
My Community

Time
Three weeks
Teaching points
Regular possessives (1st, 2nd and 3rd person)
animate and inanimate
Weather terms
Community buildings — locative review
Materials needed
● Sand table, small blocks of wood to represent houses and other village buildings, accessories for village construction and ''weather'' conditions as mentioned in lessons.
● Large cardboard cutouts to represent local buildings, such as the school, the store, the church. If these are cut from Bristol board, they can be leaned against the blackboard for use in action chains, etc.
● Real articles that belong to the children. Try to select about half animate and half inanimate objects. Since the purpose of these is to teach possession rather than new vocabulary, use articles whose names are already familiar wherever possible (for example, ball, chair, etc.).

Language

34. **Tommy's house**
Janie's house
My house, your house

35. Geographical terms suitable to local situation (for example, hill, river, lake, etc., depending on what is found in your community)

Suggested Activities

34. Paint each block of wood to conform to the colour of the children's houses. (Tempera paint works well on wood, but should be coated with shellac or urethane to keep paint from smearing.)
(a) Ask: Where is Tommy's (etc.) house?
(b) Ask: Is this Janie's house?
(c) Puppet or teacher can ask the children: Where is your house? Here, there. Teacher can ask children: Where is my house?
(d) Teacher can ask: What is this? (Pointing to a house). Pupil may reply: My house. Your house. Sam's house.

35. Arrange the sand table according to the geographic area of your community. Pieces of blue paper could be used for water; mound the sand for hills, etc. Do this arrangement as the children watch, talking about your actions. Repeat the chosen geographical terms often as you talk. Add the children's houses. Say: Put Susan's house here (there, etc.).

36. Possessive forms
    (a) Children's articles, inanimate
    (b) Children's articles, animate
    (c) Mix inanimate and animate forms

36. Collect various articles from the children and place them in two separate piles, one for inanimate articles and one for animate articles.
    (a) Bring my_____.
          your_____.
          Jean's_____.
    (b) Bring my_____.
          your_____.
          Barbara's_____.
    (c) Put two piles together and ask for above articles in random order.

37. Other buildings
    Store
    School
    Church
    Others (only the most important ones, from the child's point of view).

37. Using the large cupboard cutouts, add buildings one at a time, and practise the locative forms with each one, as you go.
    For example:
    He's going to the store.
    He's at the store.
    He's in the store.
    Is he in the store?

38. Integration

38. Make little pipecleaner men, one to represent each child in the class. Call them by the children's names. "Walk" them around the village asking:
    Who is at John's house? Sally.
    Who is (walking) on the road? Me, you.
    Where is Tommy? At the river, here, there.
    What's his name? Richard.
    Who is this? Alice, me, etc.
    Where is Sam's mother? At the lake, here, there.

39. Weather words
    (a) **It's raining**
    (b) **It's snowing**
    (c) **It's windy**
    (d) **It's a nice day**

39. "Make weather" for the village:
    (a) Use a clothes sprinkler.
    (b) Use soapflakes or detergent flakes.
    (c) Use electric fan, or just blow.
    (d) Use a big, happy-looking cardboard sun.
    Note: In planning this unit, it would likely be best to spread the weather terms out, a few days apart. Don't teach them all at once.

40. Locative review

40. (a) Using a toy animal, "walk" him around the village saying:
    He is going to John's house.
    He is going to the lake.
    He is going around the store.
    He is near the hill, etc.
    (b) Ask above sentences as questions to get yes/no answers.

41. Action chain (integration)

41. Set the cardboard buildings up around the room. Devise as many varied action chains as you can, from previous lessons.
For example: Go to the store. Bring potatoes. Put away the potatoes. Thank you.
For example: Go to the church. Sit down. Stand up. Turn around. Bring Tommy's sweater. Go to the school.

42. Weather (drill):
It's cold
It's hot

42. If children are used to thermometers, two cardboard thermometers can be coloured to show cold and hot. If this is not meaningful to them, demonstrate meanings (perhaps with puppet) by shivering, etc.
Now that some weather terms are known, try to drill these by mentioning today's weather at the beginning of every day's lesson, for the next few weeks, at least.

43. Possessive forms (integration)

43. (a) Place a few articles from Section 36 behind the cardboard buildings, one article behind each building. Ask: Where is Sally's doll? In the school. Where is Richard's ball? In the store. Where is my book? In the school, etc.
(b) Place articles in view, around room. Ask: Where is your lunchbox? Here, there, etc.
(c) Hold up one article at a time. Ask: Is this Sam's chair? Yes, no.

Church: Unit 6

School: Unit 6

Store: Unit 6

Sun: Unit 6

Post Office: Enrichment

Dock: Unit 9

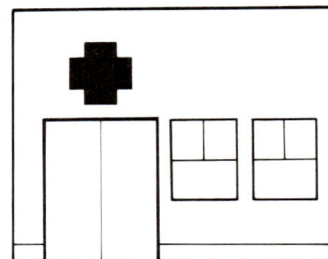

Clinic: Unit 9

Band Hall: Unit 9

If possible, make your own drawings to look like the buildings in your community. These drawings are intended only as ideas. Buildings should be *at least* two feet wide when enlarged.

Unit 7
The Clothes I Wear

Time
Two weeks
Teaching points
TA and TI verbs and/or noun incorporation
Materials needed
● Children's own outdoor clothing, other articles of children's clothing as specified for lessons, clothes-line, clothespegs, toy money, toy washtub and scrubbing board.

Language	**Suggested Activities**
44. **Put on, take off** **Your mittens** **Your hat** **Your coat** **Your boots**	44. Have class bring their outer clothing from the cloakroom to their seats. Have them put on and take off the various articles on demand. (Some children may enjoy playing teacher, and telling the others to do these things once the expressions are well learned.)
45. **My, your, his** **Clothing**	45. Put clothing belonging to various children together in a pile. If possible, include animate, inanimate, singular and plural articles. (a) Ask: Whose_____is this? Mine, yours, his. (b) Ask: What is this? My coat, your mittens, his hat, etc.
46. Verb, **buy** **Pants** **Shirt** **Dress**	46. Dramatize a store situation (use the cardboard store from Unit 6, and play money). My father goes to the store. He buys a coat. My sister goes to the store. She buys some mittens. I go to the store (puppet could say this). I buy a hat, etc.
47. Verbs **Wash** (laundry) **Hang** (to dry) Other articles of clothing as appropriate	47. Dramatize laundry day (use toy laundry tub, clothes-line, etc.). (a) My mother is washing socks (mittens, etc.). (b) My mother is washing my socks. (c) My mother is washing my brother's socks. (d) Go through (a), (b) and (c) sentence types again, using the verb "hang" (to dry).
48. **This, that, these, those**	48. Similar to Section 45, but this time, ask: Which is your coat? This, that. Which are my boots? These, those. (Try to use both animate and inanimate articles in this construction.)
49. Integration (a) Imperatives (b) Interrogatives (c) Locatives (d) Kinship (e) Negatives	49. Use vocabulary from Unit 7 in a variety of structures. (a) Wash my socks! (b) Are these your boots? Is this Tommy's hat? (c) Where is my coat? (d) Who is buying pants? My brother, etc. (e) This isn't my dress, etc.

50. **Our** (inclusive)

50. (a) Using washtub, demonstrate again 1st, 2nd, and 3rd person singular possessives, for example:
I'm washing my shirt.
I'm washing your shirt.
I'm washing his shirt.
Then, put in an article from everyone, and say: I'm washing *our* shirts.
(b) Repeat process of (a) using other articles.

Teacher's Note: For sections such as 46, 47 and 50, the simplest way to get appropriate articles of clothing might be for the children to colour and cut out articles of clothing, such as shirts, that would then be called theirs. These paper shirts may be "washed", "hung to dry", etc.

Language Note on Verb and Noun Incorporation: There are wide differences from one dialect to the next about which sentences incorporate nouns and which do not. For any sentence in your dialect for which there is a choice — for instance, if you can say either: I'm putting on *my coat* (TI verb), or, I'm put-*coat*-on-ing (incorporated) — it is probably better to teach the incorporated form. Before beginning, go over the whole unit to decide which way you will say each sentence, then be consistent by always saying it the same way.

Unit 8

Time
Three weeks
Teaching points
Consolidation
Body parts
Materials needed
- Talking book: The Morning Book (See page 43)
- Blanket or sheet

Language

51. Talking book

52. Body parts (select no more than 10)

53. Verb forms

Suggested Activities

51. (a) Go over the talking book a number of times until children are familiar with it.
(b) Dramatize the book, in sections, and expand vocabulary if children seem to handle it easily (for example, I'm painting a house, boat, box, tree, could be extended to include other articles children like to paint).
Note: Do *not*, however, extend counting past three!

52. What's this? My head, your head, his head, etc. A possible approach to drilling these forms is a game "Under the blanket". A child crawls under a blanket spread on the floor, and raises one part of his body. Children must guess: Is it your (his) foot? Is it your (his) knee? etc. This game will also give opportunities to practise negatives and interrogatives.

53. In The Morning Book there are a number of verbs with a 1st person subject. Devise interesting ways to use these verbs in their 2nd and 3rd person singular forms, interrogatives and negatives. Following are examples.
(a) If the pet used in Unit 4 is still available, body parts that use the same vocabulary for humans and animals could be reviewed with the pet. Or, a picture of that animal could be used. For example: He's washing his face (hands, nose, etc.).
Is he hungry? No, he's not hungry. He's already finished eating.
(b) During painting activities, etc., the following phrases may be used:
What are you painting? What is he painting?
Are you painting a house? Is he finished? Yes, no.
Does he want to paint? Yes, no.
I like painting. Do you like painting? Yes, no.
Does he like painting? etc.
(c) Repeat game from Unit 3, Section 16, adding:
George catches the ball. Does George catch the ball? George doesn't catch the ball, etc.

Unit 9
Community Helpers

Time
Three weeks

Teaching points
Negative imperatives
Consolidation of first eight units

Materials needed
- Pictures of Community Helpers.
- Dress-up items for above, such as: doctor's bag, nurse's cap, glasses, storekeeper's apron, etc.

Note: This is a consolidation unit — that is, the purpose is to review all the structures and vocabulary of the first eight units, using new situations. The left-hand columns below list items for consolidation (numbers refer to sections where they were taught) and the right-hand columns suggest possible ways to present the work. The success of this unit, however, and the thoroughness with which the work is covered depend on the careful planning and active imagination of the teacher.

Language

The Bus Driver
54. Vocabulary:
Bus driver
Bus
Get on, get off.
Sit down, sit still.
Here we go.
Here we are.
55. Negative imperatives:
Don't stand up.
Don't open the window.
Don't open the door.
Don't touch it.
Don't kick the seat.
56. Structure consolidation
(numbers refer to sections):
Geographical terms, 35
Weather, 39, 42
Buildings, 37
You, me, him, 3
_____'s house, 34

The Pilot

Suggested Activities

Show picture of bus driver and teach the word. Set up a "bus" by placing chairs in rows, with a rope around the outside of the "bus", showing space for door. The teacher can be the bus driver (wear a cap). Use a hoop for steering wheel.

Dramatize a bus ride with the children, using vocabulary and negative imperatives from the left-hand column, or others, as they seem suitable. Have children look out bus "windows" to notice hills, lakes, buildings, etc., as you drive along. Notice weather. Ask: Who gets off here? You, me, him, etc.

Note: Do not teach both Bus Driver and Pilot. Choose whichever one of these will be more meaningful to the children. Proceed in a similar way for either one.

The Storekeeper

57. Vocabulary:
Storekeeper
Store
Money, buy
How many?
Bag, box
Put it (him) **in the bag, box.**

58. Negative imperatives:
Don't touch it (him).
Don't drop it (him).
Don't forget it (him) (that is,
don't leave behind).
Don't slam the door.

59. Structure consolidation
(numbers refer to sections):
Bring (plus animate and
inanimate objects), **7, 8, 9, 11**
Clothing, **44–47**
Locatives, **13, 40**
Toys, **14**
Put the_____on the_____, **12**
Put away the_____, **12**

Show picture of storekeeper and teach the word. Set up a store, with toys and clothing to sell. Let one of the children be the storekeeper. He can wear an apron, or blazer, or store-pin — whatever local storekeepers wear — and teacher can come in to buy things, using vocabulary from Section 57. Exchange and let teacher be storekeeper and pupil be customer, to practise negative imperatives from Section 58. Storekeeper could have an assistant, to put to use some of the structures, such as bring, put away, put_____on_____, etc. Possibly customers could use the toy and clothing vocabulary to indicate what they want to buy.

The Nurse and the Doctor

60. Vocabulary:
Doctor, nurse
He is sick.
What's the matter?
Swallow pills.
He is fine.
He drinks water.
He is feverish.
Roll up your sleeve.
He takes care of him.
He sneezes.
He coughs.

61. Negative imperatives:
Don't get up (out of bed).
Don't cry.
Don't be scared.
Don't go outside.
Don't open your mouth.

62. Structure consolidation
(numbers refer to sections):
Name, **1**
Yes, no, **2**
Imperatives, **4, 16**
Here, there, **5**

Warning: If in this section you give out candy ''pills'', it is important to work with the classroom teacher to plan a safety lesson for the children. Be sure the children are warned *not* to play with real medicine in their homes: that doing so could have serious consequences.

Show pictures of doctor and nurse and teach these words.
(a) Let puppet go to nurse for a needle (teacher is nurse); then let other children come for needles (Nurse can say: don't cry).
(b) Let puppet play doctor (put a white coat on him and have him examine the children, saying: I'm going to look at your_____(leg, arm, etc.).
(c) Set up a play hospital, with a nurse to record names, ask what's the matter, etc., and a doctor to give out pills, bandage fingers, etc. Beds can be made by rolling out butcher paper lengths on the floor. Toy thermometer can elicit: ''Don't open your mouth.''
(d) Nurse can give puppet an eye test (saying: Do you see it?) and an ear test (Do you hear it?) for practice with 1 and 2 on 3 (subject-object combinations).

Subject-object combinations
1 and 2 on 3, 31, 32, 33
Body parts, 52
AI verbs, 17—20, 23, 24, 28

(e) Have class pretend to cough, sneeze, etc., for practice with AI verbs: James is coughing; The boys are sneezing, etc.

The Teacher

63. Vocabulary:
Teacher
School
Children
He plays.
He paints.
He reads.
He rings the bell.

Show pictures of men and women teachers, and teach the words. Review sections from The Morning Book in which children are at school. Let children dramatize a school day, where one child, acting as teacher, rings the bell, and others do as children did in The Morning Book. Dress-up items for teacher could include wearing glasses frames, or carrying a pointer. "Teacher" can get class to count to three, stand up, sit down, etc. Ask yes/no questions, such as: Are the boys painting? Is Sally ringing the bell? Is Jamie sick?

64. Structure consolidation (numbers refer to sections):
Kinship, 25, 27, 29
"The Morning Book" review, 51
This, that, these, those, 48
Counting to three.

65. Extra practice
(a) 3rd person plurals practice

65. (a) This form is easy to neglect. It was introduced in Unit 4, Section 24, and needs to be maintained. Some possibilities in this unit:
The boys are feverish.
The nurses are getting into the plane (the bus).
My sisters are sick.
The pilots are in the store.
Note: Do not teach sentences like the above in isolation. Always work out a "situation" where an utterance will be appropriate.

(b) Locatives practice

(b) Place cardboard buildings (Section 41, Unit 6) around the room. Place pictures of doctor, pilot, etc., and pictures of family members behind the various buildings.
Ask: Where is the pilot? Where is your grand-mother?, etc.
Answers: In the store, etc. Here, there.
Note: You may wish to add a few more locations at this time, such as the hospital (or clinic), band hall, dock (for plane), etc. Use only those locations appropriate to *your* community. See drawings, Unit 6, page 24.

(c) 3rd person on 4th person practice

(c) Ensure that the children have had a lot of listening practice with forms such as these:
He goes with him.
He buys it, him.
He sees (looks at, takes care of) him.
He takes a pill.
He drinks water.

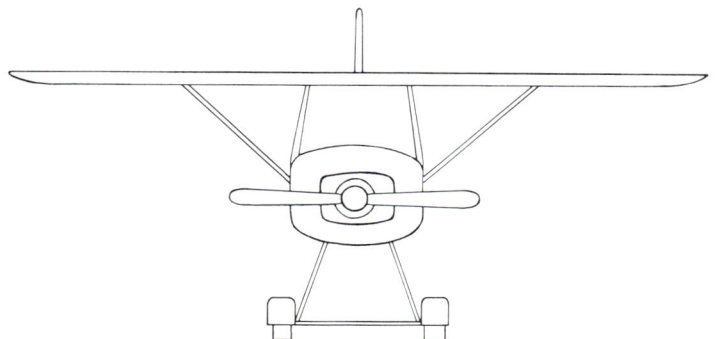

Unit 10
Let's Put On a Play

Time
Four weeks
Teaching points
The voluntive
The past tense
The diminutive
Materials needed
- Talking book: Little Girl and the Three Bears (See page 47).
- Properties for presenting this as a play.
- Noun chart (see drawings, page 50).
- Verb chart (see drawings, page 51).

Language

66. Talking book

67. Noun chart

68. The play

69. Verb chart

70. Invite a guest or guests: **Do you want to come_____?**

71. Serve the guest or guests cookies and juice.

Suggested Activities

66. (a) Go through the talking book several times until children are familiar with it.
(b) Let various children act out the small segments of the story.

67. (a) In the noun chart pictures, ask children to show you the chairs, bowls, etc.
(b) Ask children to show you a chair, a little chair, a big chair, etc.

68. Present the whole play. Since there are only four actors, you may wish to have a number of "casts" so that more children can take part. "Extra" children may also be used to help with properties, or act as trees (hold leaves in hands, hold arms up) in the forest where the bears go walking. Remember, the main point is language practice, not dramatic excellence. If the children wish to speak their parts, encourage them to do so. If they are shy, use the tape recording of the talking book while they act it out.

69. Have children point to the appropriate picture in the verb chart for each utterance:
The bear wants to eat. The bear is eating.
The baby wants to sleep. The baby is sleeping, etc.
(Cover and omit reference to past tense pictures.)

70. Invite the principal, or another class, or the childrens' mothers to come and see the play. Use every occasion to employ the voluntive form: Do you want to come?, etc.

71. Before the day of the presentation, have the children practise serving cookies and juice, asking: Do you want to drink milk (or juice, or tea)? Do you want to eat cookies?

72. Past tense forms

72. After the presentation, talk with the class about what happened, using the past tense. For example: Your mother ate a cookie. Mr. Brown drank some juice. Martha brought the cups.

73. Verb chart

73. Continue study as in Section 70, this time including the past tense pictures in the verb chart: The bear wants to eat. The bear is eating. The bear ate.

Unit 11
What Do Things Do?

Time
Two weeks
Teaching points
Review four verb types
Materials needed
● About 10 articles to be tested (such as: pencil, plastic toy, pin, piece of cardboard, fork, etc.). In selecting articles, two things should be considered: (1) about half should be animate and half inanimate, (2) every test should have at least one (and preferably more than one) object that tests positively.
● The equipment to be used for testing: floating (basin of water, for example), bending, breaking or tearing, smelling (no equipment needed), clinging (magnet), burning (matches or lighter and fireproof container).
Note: If there is a science room in the school, it should be able to help you find much of this equipment.

Language

74. **Is the____going to float?**
Yes, or no, it will, won't float.
Is the ____floating?
Yes, no, it's, it's not, floating.
Did the____float?
Yes, no, it did, didn't, float.

75. Perform the other tests, one at a time

76. Game: **What is it?**

77. Transitive forms

78. Plural forms

Suggested Activities

74. Work with one test at a time. Have the children test all the articles, one after another, for floating.

75. Follow same pattern as in Section 75, for bending, breaking, etc.

76. Hide an article under a box and tell the children one or more of its characteristics. For example: it floats, it breaks, what is it? Let them guess, until they guess correctly (answer: a pencil).

77. As you work with each test, include as many transitive forms as possible. For example: the pencil breaks; Johnny breaks the pencil. Include interrogative and negative forms of the transitive verbs as well.

78. Group two or more articles together. For example: the pencils float; the papers tear, etc.
Warning: Again, as in Unit 9, it would be wise to get the cooperation of the classroom teacher to ensure the children have a safety lesson on the use of matches.

Talking Book:*
Where's Kitty?
(Unit 3)

1

2

3

4

*See instructions on page 8 for preparing a talking book.

5

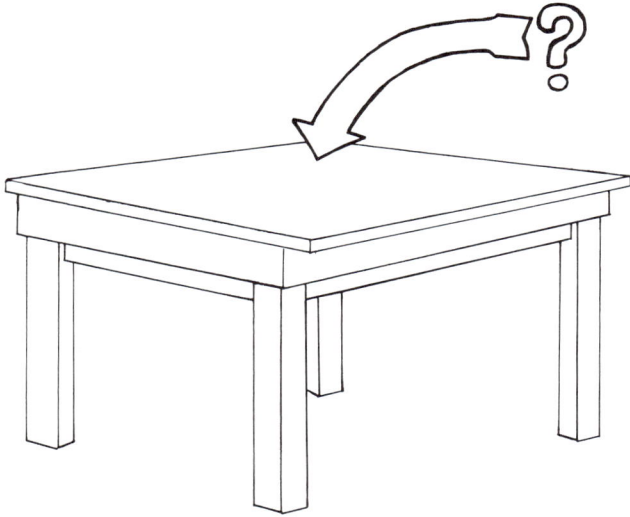

6

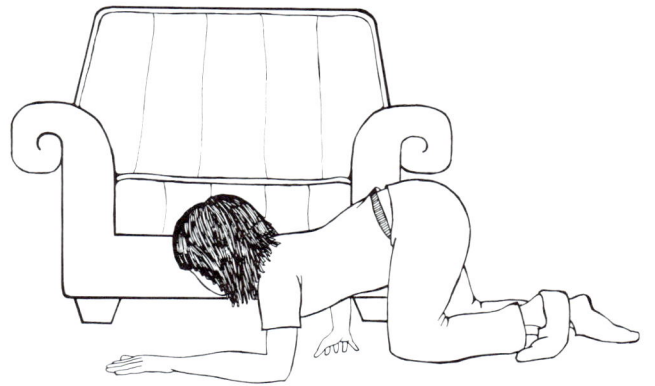

7

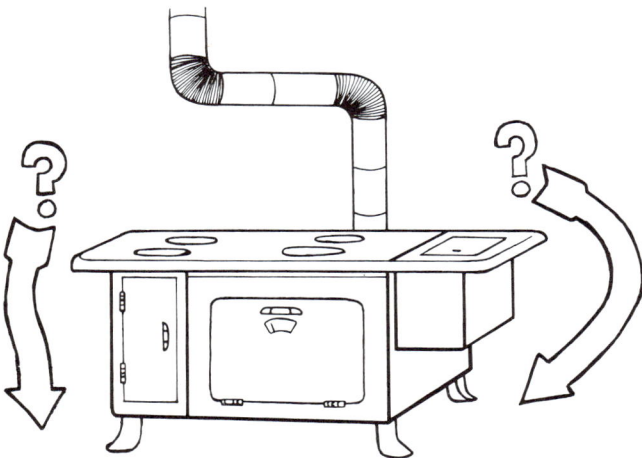

8

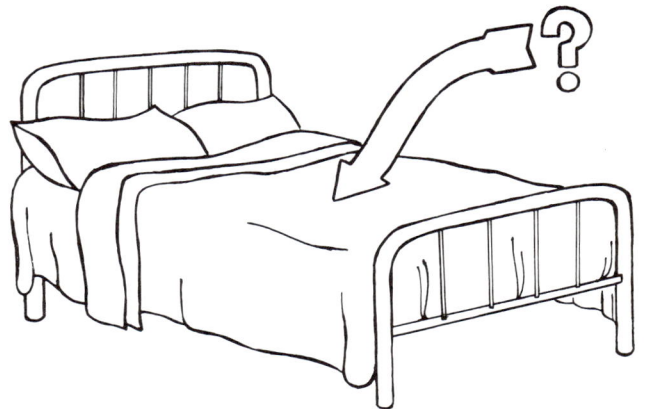

9

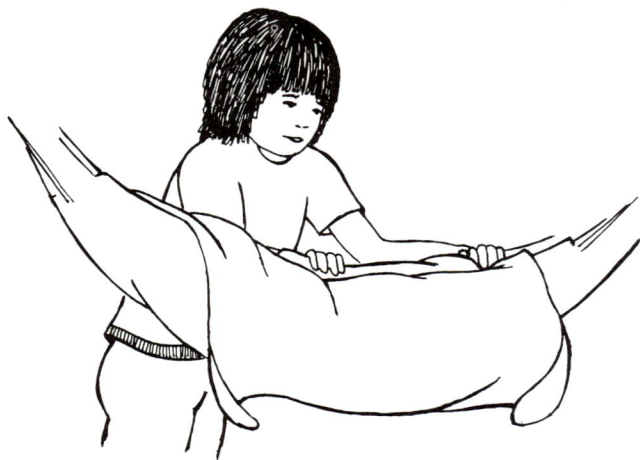

10

11

Tape Script

1. Where's Kitty? (Cover title)
2. Kitty, here's food. Come and eat.
3. Where are you?
4. Behind the cupboard? No!
5. On the table? No!
6. Under the chair? No!
7. Near the stove? No!
8. On the bed? No!
9. In the swing?
10. Ah! Here you are!
11. Come here. Eat.

Language Note: The forms "Where are you?" (No. 3) and "Here you are!" (No. 10) might be understood by the children to mean "Where is he?" and "Here he is." To prevent misunderstanding, you might get the children to demonstrate these verbs by acting out a little game of hide-and-seek with each other, using such phrases as, "Sally, where are you?", and so on.

Talking Book:
Forest Animals
(Unit 4)

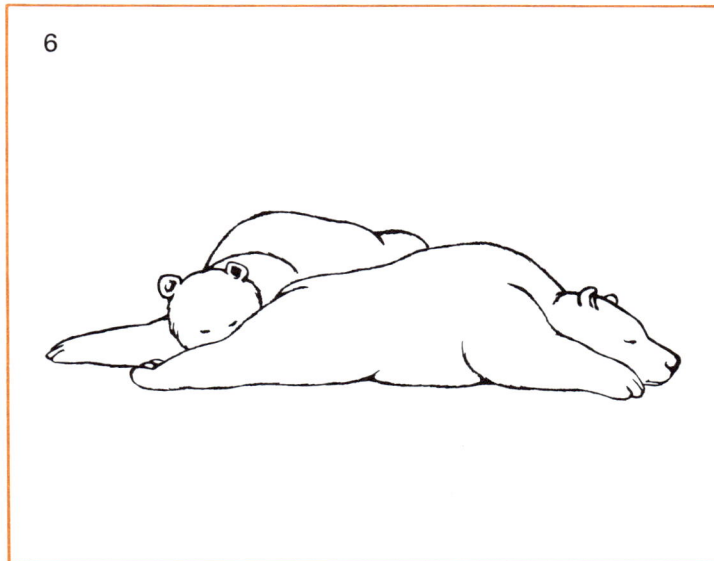

1

2

3

4

5

6

7

8

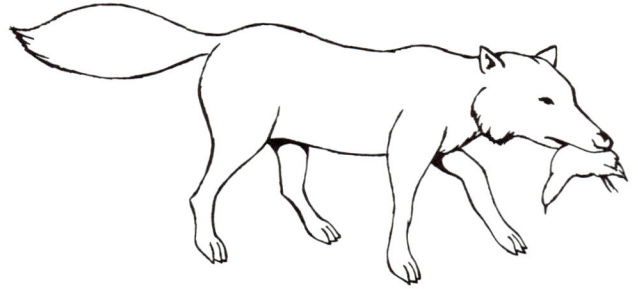

9

10

11

12

13

14

15

16

17

18

19

20

Tape Script

1. Deer (singular)
2. The deer is running.
3. The deer are running.
4. Bear
5. The bear is sleeping.
6. The bears are sleeping.
7. Fox
8. The fox is eating.
9. The foxes are eating.
10. Rabbit
11. The rabbit is going home.
12. The rabbits are going home.
13. The deer is drinking.
14. The bears are digging.
15. The fox is digging.
16. The rabbits are sleeping.
17. The deer are eating.
18. The bear is going home.
19. The foxes are drinking.
20. The rabbit is running.

Talking Book:
The Morning Book
(Unit 8)

1

2

3

4

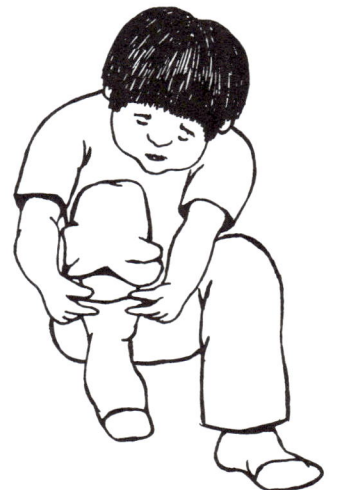

5

6

7

8

9

10

11

Tape Script

1. It's early in the morning (already morning).
   It's going to be a nice day.
2. Get up!
   O.K. I am getting up.
   I still want to sleep.
   Are you up?
   Yes, I am up.
3. Get washed!
   O.K. I'm getting washed.
   Where is the soap? Here it is!
   I am washing my face.
   I am washing my neck.
   I am washing my ears.
   I am washing my hands.
   Finished!
   Are you washed?
   Yes, I am already washed.

4. Get dressed!
   O.K. I am getting dressed.
   Where is my shirt? Here it is.
   I am putting on my socks.
   I am putting on my pants.
   I am putting on my shoes.
   Finished!
   Are you dressed?
   Yes, I am already dressed.

5. Come and eat!
   O.K. I am hungry.
   Pass me the sugar.
   Pass me the milk.
   Pass me the eggs.
   Pass me the bread.
   Mmmm . . . it tastes good.
   I'm full.
   Have you eaten?
   Yes, I have already eaten.

6. Feed the dog!
   Here Wolf. Are you hungry?
   Here is the food. Eat!
   Did you feed the dog?
   Yes, he's eating.
   He's very hungry.
   He's already finished eating.

7. Hurry up!
   It's eight o'clock.
   Get going!
   Where's my brother (older brother)?
   Here!
   We are going now.
   Take the books.

8. Hello!
   Hello!
   Do you want to paint?
   Yes, I want to paint.
   Paint something.
   I am painting a house.
   I am painting a boat.
   I am painting a box.
   I am painting a tree.
   Are you finished?
   Yes, I am finished.
   Here is my painting.
   Good!

9. The bell is ringing. Let's play!
   Where is the ball?
   Here it is.
   One, two, three! Catch it!
   I caught it.
   One, two, three! Catch it!
   I caught it.
   One, two, three! Catch it!
   No, I did not catch it. (I missed it).
   Get the ball.
   Here it is.
   One, two, three! Catch it!
   The bell is ringing .
   Let's go in.
   Let's go.

10. Do you want to read?
    O.K. I want to read.
    Where is the book?
    Here it is.
    I like to read.
    I like stories.
    I like books.
    Are you finished?
    Yes, I am finished.

11. Let's go home.
    See you later.

Note on Preparing Tape: If possible, get a number of people to help when you record this tape. Dramatize, with different voices for mother, child, teacher, and other children. Including such sound effects as a dog barking (Section 6), a bell ringing (Section 9), etc., will add to the interest of the book.

Talking Book:
Little Girl and the Three Bears (Unit 10)

13

14

15

16

17

18

19

20

21

22

23

24

Tape Script

1. My porridge is too hot.
2. Me too, my porridge is too hot.
3. Me too, my porridge is too hot.
4. I want to walk in the woods.
5. Me too, I want to walk in the woods.
6. Me too, I want to walk in the woods.
7. Oh! A little house! I want to go in.
8. I want to eat.
9. The porridge is too hot.
10. This one, too, the porridge is too hot.
11. This one's fine.
12. I want to sit down.
13. This chair is too big.
14. This chair is too big, too.
15. Oh! The chair broke.
16. I want to sleep.
17. The bed is too hard.
18. The bed is too soft.
19. This one's fine.
20. Somebody messed up my porridge.
21. Me too, somebody messed up my porridge.
22. Somebody ate all my porridge.
23. Somebody sat in my chair.
24. Me too, somebody sat in my chair.
25. Somebody broke my chair.
26. Somebody messed up my bed.
27. Me too, somebody messed up my bed.
28. Somebody is sleeping in my bed.
29. What's your name?
30. I want to go home.

Noun Charts
(Unit 10)

50

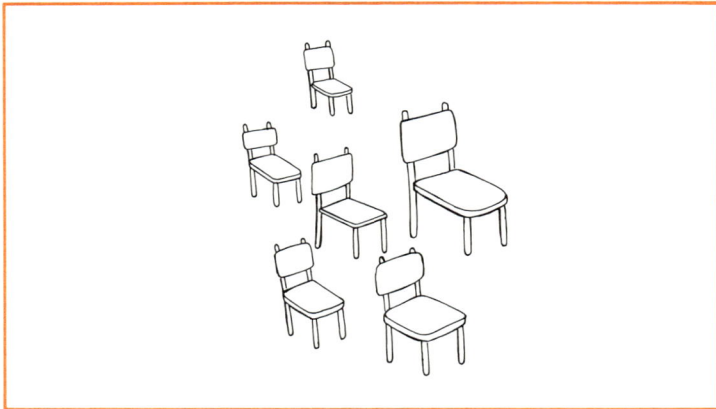

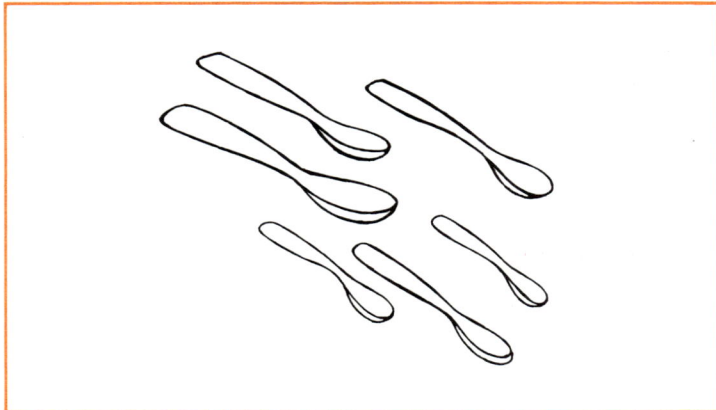

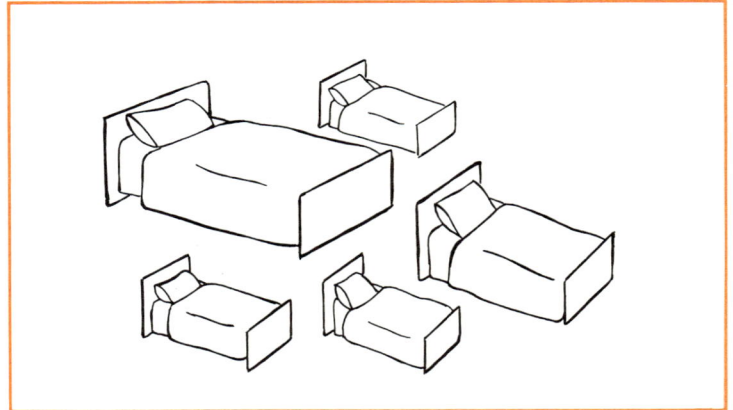

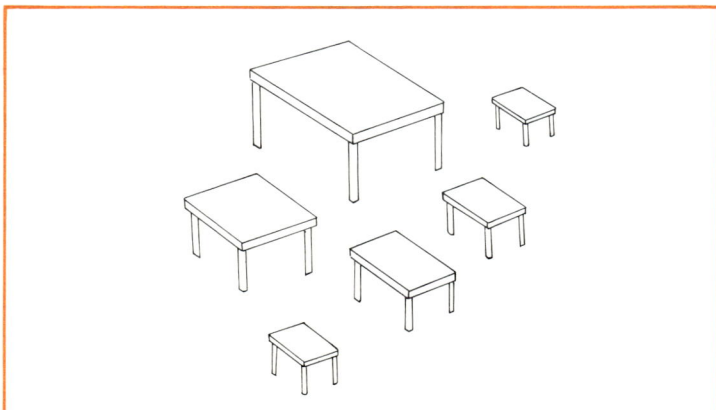

Verb Charts
(Unit 10)

Instructions for Making a Verb Chart

From these 14 sets of pictures, choose six
sets. In choosing, be sure that the same verb,
used in the

voluntive	present	past

Enlarge the sets of your choice, and arrange
on a chart like this:

voluntive

present

past

is the suitable and natural one to use in your
dialect.

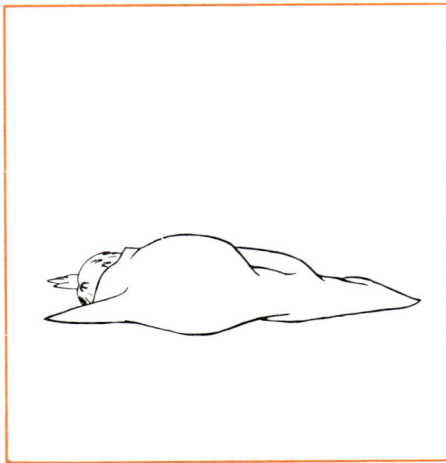

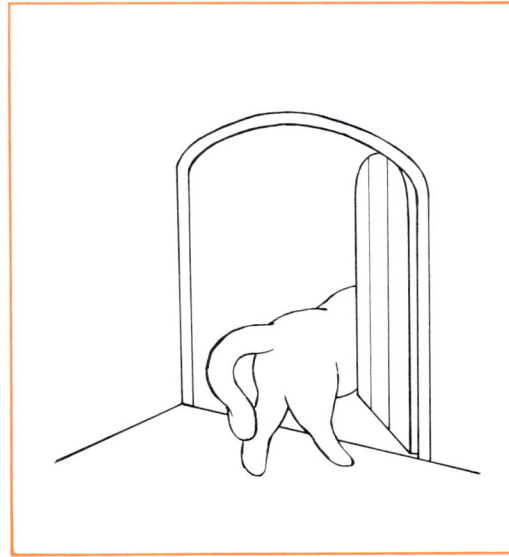

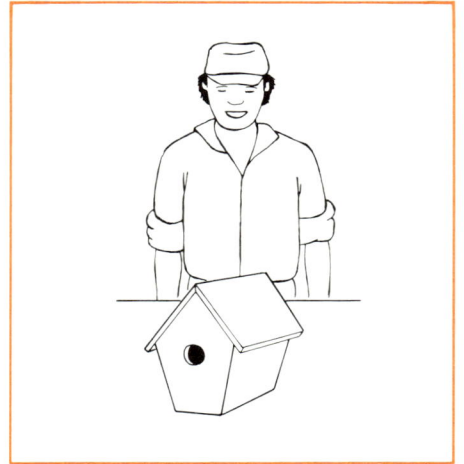

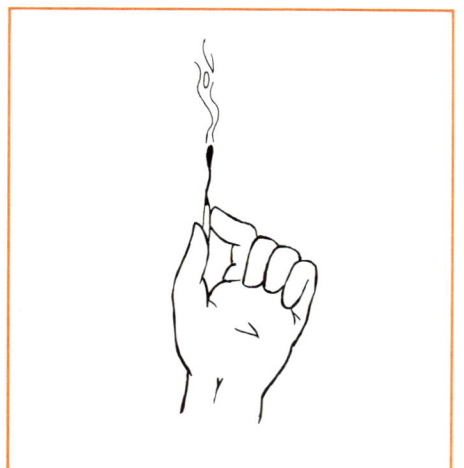

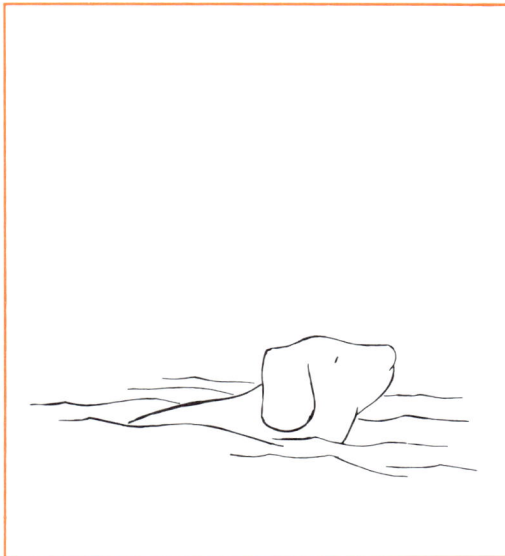

List of Teaching Materials for the Kindergarten Course

Unit 1
Hand puppet
Penny

Unit 2
Paper plates and cups
Plastic knives, forks, spoons
Magazine pictures of food *or* play food

Unit 3
Box of toys (miscellaneous)
Large rubber ball
Talking book: Where's Kitty, page 36

Unit 4
Live pet in a cage
Pet needs
Talking book: Forest Animals, page 39

Unit 5
Large sheets of newsprint, tempera paint,
large brushes
Dress-up clothes
Peep show made from shoebox
Family photos children brought from home

Unit 6
Sand table
Small blocks of wood painted to represent
local buildings
Large cardboard pictures of buildings, page 24
Pipecleaner figures
Small toy dog — scale of sand table model
Construction paper (blue lake, green trees,
etc.)
Cardboard sun, page 24
Clothes sprinkler
Detergent flakes

Unit 7
Various articles of children's own clothing
Clothesline, clothespegs
Toy laundry tub and scrubbing board
Toy money

Unit 8
Blanket or sheet
Talking book: The Morning Book, page 43

Unit 9
School bell (real or toy)
Roll of butcher paper
Pictures of Community Helpers page 31
Picture of bus, or plane
Cash register (toy)
Candy pills
Dress-up items

Unit 10
Talking book: Little Girl and the Three Bears,
page 47
Noun chart pictures, page 50
Verb chart pictures, page 51
Bowls and other properties for play
(available in classroom)

Unit 11
Basin of water
Magnet
Matches and fireproof container

List of Language Structures for the Kindergarten Course

(Numbers refer to sections unless otherwise indicated.)

Verbs — Independent Order

II (weather), 39, 42
II (general), Unit 11
AI, 17, 24, Unit 11
TI, 32, 33
TA (direct forms), 31, 33
TA (with indirect object), 16
Negative forms, 19, 20
Interrogative forms (yes/no questions), 18
Voluntive, 69, 70, 71
Past tense, 72, 73

Verbs — Imperative Order

AI, 4
TI, 8, 9, 11, 12
TA, 7, 9, 11, 12
Negative forms, Unit 9

Pronouns

Personal, 3
Demonstratives, 48
Possessives, 45
Here, there, 5

Nouns

Possessives (body parts), 52
Possessives (kinship terms), 25, 27, 29
Possessives (regular), 45
Diminutives, 67
Locatives, 13, 14, 27, 40
Incorporation possibilities, 44, 46, 47, 51

Glossary

Active Knowledge
The ability to speak the language being taught. This ability follows a passive knowledge of the language.

AI Verbs
Animate, intransitive. The subject of the verb is animate and the verb is intransitive.

Animate (see *gender*)

A—V Materials (audio-visual)
Materials that help the teacher teach by means of the pupils' ears (tapes, records, etc.) or eyes (pictures, films, charts, etc.).

Conjunct
An order of the verb in Algonkian languages in which the verb does not stand alone, but in conjunction with another main element. Used in many ways, such as in subordinate clauses, content questions, etc.

Consolidation
Using material just learned in a variety of ways in order to make it become familiar.

Core Program
Program in which a period of time (usually daily) is set aside to teach the second language.

Course of Studies
Written program which tells what to teach and in what order to teach it. Sometimes such courses will also give suggestions on *how* to teach the material.

Curriculum
The total of all things that go into the teaching of any subject: teacher's knowledge, materials, course of studies, activities, teaching methods, etc.

Diminutive
The form of a noun which indicates smallness.

Dubitative
A form of the verb in Algonkian languages which expresses the possibility of doubt.

Exclusive
Term used to describe the 1st person plural form of the verb when the person being spoken to is *excluded* from the action of the verb (such as, he and I).
Compare *inclusive.*

First Language
The language a child learns first (from the time he is born until he is ready to begin school).

Gender
The structural class to which a noun belongs. The gender of a noun often affects other parts of speech with which it has to do.

Gender — Animate
A class of nouns in Algonkian languages including all living things, and other things that are *classified* as living.

Gender — Inanimate
A class of nouns in Algonkian languages which include all things not *classified* as living.

II Verbs
Inanimate, intransitive. The subject of the verb is inanimate, and the verb is intransitive.

Imperative
The order of the verb in which commands are given.

Implications for Utterance
The probability that for any piece of language taught, the student will have occasion to *use* that piece of language outside the classroom. One test of good lesson material is that the IFU be 80% or higher.

Inanimate (see *gender*)

Inclusive
Term used to describe the 1st person plural form of the verb when the person being spoken to is *included* in the action of the verb (such as you and I). Compare *exclusive.*

Incorporation of the Noun
A form of the verb in which the noun object of the verb is incorporated, or placed right into the middle of the verb as a part of it. For instance, in most Algonkian languages, the noun "coat" is usually incorporated into the verb in the sentence "Put on your coat."

Independent
An order of the verb in Algonkian languages in which the verb stands alone (for contrast, see *conjunct*).

Integration
Joining and applying material just learned to material already known.

Intentive (see *voluntive*)

Interrogative
The form which asks a question.

Intransitive
A verb that does not take an object. For instance: Eat! (or) He ate. (Compare with *transitive* examples.)

Kinship Terms
Words used to identify people who are related, such as, my father, her aunt, etc.

Locative
The form of a noun that indicates location, such as, on the table, in the lake, etc.

Negative
The form which indicates "not" or "don't", such as, he's not sick; don't go away.

Obviative
The *second* 3rd person. For example, in the sentence "Jake shot the moose who staggered and fell on him", "Jake" and "him" are 3rd person forms, and "moose" and "who" are 4th person (or obviative) forms.

Passive Knowledge
Ability to understand the language being taught. The ability precedes an active knowledge of the language.

Pattern (see *structure*)
A meaningful arrangement of words which recur systematically, and may allow for word substitution. In the pattern "the ____ house", the blank could be filled by: green, little, brick, etc., and house could be changed to many other nouns.

Pejorative
The form of a noun which indicates that the noun is unattractive or undesirable.

Person
1st (me), 2nd (you), 3rd (him), 4th (the other him).

Plural
More than one.

Preterit
An aspect of the verb showing action in the past that was intended but unrealized, or that was cut off and no longer occurs, or that happened in the remote past.

Pronouns — Demonstrative
This, that, these, those.

Pronouns — Personal
I, you, he, she, we, they, me, him, her, them.

Pronouns — Possessive
My, your, his, her, our, their.

Questions — Content
Questions beginning with words such as who, what, where, when, why, how, etc., must use the conjunct order.

Questions — Yes / No
Questions that can be answered by saying yes or no may use the independent order.

Rote Counting
Counting one, two, three, etc., without reference to what is being counted.

Second Language
The language a child learns after he can speak his first language.

Singular
One

Structure — Language Structure
The way a language works, such as, the way words fit together, etc.

Structure (see *pattern*)

Subject—Object Combinations
For example: 1 on 3 = I see him; 2 on 1 = you see me; 3 on 4 = he sees him.

Substitution
Replacing one word with another in a place where it fits. For example: the *cat* is black; the *dog* is black. Dog is a substitution for cat.

TA Verbs
Transitive, animate. The verb is transitive, and the object of the verb is animate.

TI Verbs
Transitive, inanimate. The verb is transitive, and the object of the verb is inanimate.

Transitive
A verb that takes an object. For instance, eat the fish (the object is *fish*, so eat is transitive). He ate it (the object is *it*, so ate is transitive. (Compare with *intransitive* examples.)

Vocabulary
The words that are used (such as cat, walk, big, etc.) in contrast to *structure* items such as "s" in cats, "est" in biggest, "ed" in walked, etc.

Voluntive
Also called intentive. Form of the verb that expresses desire, intention, or future time. Usually expressed by the syllable "wi".